Starting Off with Role Play and Discussion

これからの英語コミュニケーション講座

NAN'UN-DO

このテキストの音声を無料で視聴（ストリーミング）・ダウンロードできます。自習用音声としてご活用ください。
以下のサイトにアクセスしてテキスト番号で検索してください。

https://nanun-do.com　テキスト番号 [**511960**]

※ 無線 LAN（WiFi）に接続してのご利用を推奨いたします。
※ 音声ダウンロードは Zip ファイルでの提供になります。
　お使いの機器によっては別途ソフトウェア（アプリケーション）の導入が必要となります。

※ Starting Off with Role Play and Discussion 音声ダウンロードページは以下の QR コードからもご利用になれます。

Acknowledgments: The author wants to thank Phillip Norton, Joseph Cronin, Jim Knudsen and Mikiko Hirata who gave valuable feedback on the activities in this textbook.

Starting Off with Role Play and Discussion
これからの英語コミュニケーション講座

Copyright © 2019
By
Eric Bray

All Rights Reserved.
No part of this book may be reproduced in any form without written permission from the author and Nan'un-do Co., Ltd.

Message to Students

Greetings! And welcome to *Starting Off with Role Play and Discussion*. This textbook has been created to help you get started with role play and discussion activities that will help you take your English to the next level. These activities are especially designed to give you a chance to practice the English you will need to succeed in situations you may find yourself in when traveling abroad. During the role plays relax and let yourself go a bit. Try to imagine what it would be like to actually be the person in the role you are playing. Think about the language, attitude, body language, and tone of voice the person would use. But, importantly, remember to keep the "play" in these role play activities. Enjoy!

Useful Expressions for Discussions

Giving your opinion
I think ...
In my opinion ...
The way I see it ...
If you ask me ...

Agreeing
I agree.
I think so too.
You're right.
Definitely.

Agreeing + but
I agree, but ...
I think so, too, but ...
You're right, but ...
Yes, but ...

Disagreeing
I don't agree. I think ...
Sorry, I disagree. In my opinion ...
I'm afraid I don't agree.
Possibly, but ...
No way!

Clarifying
Could you repeat that, please?
Sorry, I'm not sure I understand.
Could you please explain?
What do you mean by ...?
Do you mean ...?

General comments
Hmm ... That's interesting.
I never thought of that.
I see ... Very interesting.
That's a good point.

TABLE OF CONTENTS

Unit

1	You and Your Classmates	6
2	You, Going Out to Eat	11
3	You, Shopping	16
4	You, Out on the Town	20
5	You, Planning a Trip	25
6	You, Hotel Guest	29
7	You, World Traveler	35
8	You, Living with Others	39
9	You, Job Hunting	45
10	You, Giving Good Advice	50
11	You, Solving World Problems	57
12	You, Inventor for the Future	62
13	You and Older People in Your Life	68
14	You, Making Your Own Role Play	72
15	Review and Practice	79

Unit 1

You and Your Classmates

Activity 1 Starting Off — Information Circles

Task 1 Your teacher will draw a circle on the board and put some important information about him/herself in it. Write this information in the circle below. Then ask your teacher Yes/No questions to find out why this information is important to him/her.

Useful Language

Yes/No Question Starters

Do you …?	Did you …?
Are you …?	Were you …?
Can you …?	Have you ever …?
_____	_____

Example: If your teacher writes "John" on the board, you could ask, "Is your first name John?" or "Is John your brother?" or "Do you have a son named John?"

Information About Your Teacher

| Task 2 | Now it's your turn. Write a few things about yourself in the circle below. Some of the things can be easy to guess. Try to write a couple of things that are interesting or surprising. Get together with two or three other students and show them your circle. Introduce yourself by saying, "Hi, I'm ___(your name)___. Nice to meet you." The other students should then ask you Yes/No questions about the information in your circle. Make sure that when you answer "yes," you give more information. |

Important Information about You

What did you learn about your classmates that was interesting?

I learned that ...

Activity II Learning More about Your Classmates

Task Write short answers to the questions below. Write a question of your own and answer it too. Then ask some students the questions and note down their names and one piece of information about each person below. Be sure to ask follow-up questions to make the conversation longer.

1. What do you like to do in your free time?
   _____

2. What's your favorite food?
   _____

3. Who's your favorite musician or musical group?
   _____

4. What did you do last weekend?
   _____

5. What trip do you want to take some day?
   _____

6. (your question)
   _____ / _____

Follow-Up Question

 Model Conversation

A: Hi, I'm Ryu Takamoto. Nice to meet you.
B: Nice to meet you, too. I'm Nobuhiro Ueno.
A: What do you like to do in your free time, Nobuhiro?
B: I like to watch movies.
A: Really? Me too. Have you seen any good movies lately?
B: Yeah, I saw a good movie called "La La Land" last week.

Follow-Up Questions

Follow-up questions are questions you ask to get more information after your partner has answered your first question. They can be Yes/No Questions or Information Questions that start with:
What …? Who …? Where …? How …? When …? Have you …? Why …? etc.

About Your Classmates

	Name	Information		Name	Information
1.	_____	_____	6.	_____	_____
2.	_____	_____	7.	_____	_____
3.	_____	_____	8.	_____	_____
4.	_____	_____	9.	_____	_____
5.	_____	_____	10.	_____	_____

Activity III A Famous Person — Guess Who

Task 1 Your teacher will think of a famous person but will not tell you who it is. Ask your teacher questions like those in the **Useful Language** box and write the answers in the spaces below. Then try to guess who the famous person is.

Useful Language

Is this person a man or a woman?
What's his/her nationality?
How old is he/she?
What does he/she look like?
What kind of work does he/she do?
Can you give us a hint?

Your Teacher's Famous Person

1. Male or Female? _____
2. Nationality? _____
3. Age? _____
4. Appearance (looks like)? _____
5. Job, Position? _____
6. Hints? _____

Task 2 Now think of a famous person. Make notes about him/her on the lines below (you may have to do some research on your smartphone). Also write down a couple of things that will make good hints about who the person is. Then get together with two or three other students and ask questions to find out who their famous person is. Don't give them information right away that will make it easy to guess your famous person. Save that for later when they ask you for hints.

Your Famous Person

1. Male or Female? _____
2. Nationality? _____
3. Age? _____
4. Appearance? _____
5. Job, Position? _____
6. Hints? _____
   _____

Useful Language

OK, I'm ready. Ask me some questions.
Sorry, I'll tell you that later.
Would you like a hint?

What famous people did your group members choose?

1. _____
2. _____
3. _____

Unit 2: You, Going Out to Eat

Activity I — Discuss the Topic

Task: Read and think about the questions below. Make up one question of your own. Write short answers in the spaces, and then discuss the questions in pairs or small groups.

1. When you go out to eat, what's your favorite kind of food?
   (fast food, sushi, Chinese, French, ramen, etc.)

2. How often do you go out to eat?
   (once a week, twice a month, etc.)

3. What's your favorite restaurant? Why do you like it?

4. What is a restaurant you don't like? Why?

5. Can you recommend a restaurant that has good value?
   (good value = low price and high quality)

6. When you choose a restaurant, what is more important to you – the food, the atmosphere, or the price? Why?

7. Have you ever had bad service in a restaurant? What did you do?

8. Your Question _____

Activity II Getting Ready — Can I Take Your Order?

Task Look at the Sample Menu and the **Model Conversation** below. With two or three other students, practice the conversation, taking turns being the Server. Use the Order Form below when you play the role of the Server.

Sample Menu

Paradise Bar and Grill

Appetizers	Smoked Salmon	$8	**Drinks**	Mineral water	$5
	Olives	$5		Juice (apple or orange)	$5
	Cheese Plate	$10		Wine by the glass	$8
Soups and Salads	French Onion Soup	$8		(Merlot or Chardonnay)	
	Minestrone Soup	$8		Tea or Coffee	$6
	Caesar Salad	$10	**Desserts**	Chocolate Cake	$7
	Green Salad	$6		Cheesecake	$8
Main Dishes	Roast Chicken	$16		Strawberry Ice Cream	$5
	Seafood Pasta	$16			
	Chili Shrimp	$14		* All Main Dishes come with a choice of a baked potato, rice, or bread.	
	Pizza Margherita	$12			

5

 Model Conversation

Server: Welcome to the Paradise Bar and Grill. Can I take your order?
Customer: Yes. We'll start with the Cheese Plate. Then I'll have the Roast Chicken with a bowl of French Onion Soup.
Server: OK. A Cheese Plate appetizer and then Roast Chicken with a bowl of French Onion Soup. Would you like a baked potato, rice, or French bread with your meal?
Customer: I'll have a baked potato.
Server: Sure. Now, what would you like to drink?
Customer: I'll have mineral water, please.
Server: Fine. How about some dessert tonight?
Customer: Hmmm ... Maybe I'll order dessert later.
Server: OK. How about you, sir? What will you have? (takes the other customers' orders)
OK. Let me check the order. (repeats the order)
OK. I'll be right back with your drinks.

Order Form

	Cust. 1	Cust. 2	Cust. 3
Appetizer			
Soup Salad			
Main Dish			
Potato Rice Bread			
Dessert			
Drink			

12 Unit 2

Activity III Getting Ready — Your Restaurant

Task 1 *Pretend you are going to open a new restaurant of your own. Get together with two or three other students and decide what kind of restaurant you would like to open. (Italian, sushi, izakaya, steak house, etc.). Then give your restaurant a name.*

Kind of restaurant _____

Restaurant name _____

Task 2 *With your group members, design a menu for your restaurant. Like the menu in* **Activity II**, *your menu should have separate sections for appetizers, main dishes, drinks, etc. Then practice the* **Model Conversation** *from* **Activity II** *using your restaurant's menu.*

Your Restaurant's Menu

_____
(restaurant name)

Activity IV Role Plays — At the Restaurant

Task 1 Look at the roles for customers and servers below. Add one role of your own. First, do the role plays with your group from **Activity III** using the menu you created. Take turns, with one person playing the Server and the others playing Customers. Both Servers and Customers should keep their roles secret until the end. Don't tell your group members what your role is. After the role play, ask them to guess what your role was.

Customer Roles

Situation: In a restaurant   **Roles:** Customer   Server

1. You're rude and impatient. You're in a big hurry to eat.
2. You're indecisive. You can't make up your mind.
3. You're cheap. Everything looks so expensive.
4. You're clumsy. You keep dropping and spilling things.
5. You have had too much to drink already, but you want to drink more.
6. You're nervous. It's your first date with this person.
7. You're very attracted to the waiter/waitress. You flirt with him/her.
8. Free Role — (Make up your own role. Write it here.)

Server Roles

1. You're stressed out. The restaurant is really busy today.
2. You're bossy. You try to tell the customers what to order.
3. It's your first day on the job, and you make a lot of mistakes.
4. You're a snob. You think your restaurant is too sophisticated for these customers.
5. You're very attracted to one of the customers. You flirt with him/her.
6. You're a very patient person. Nothing can bother you.
7. You're lazy. You don't really feel like working today.
8. Free Role — (Make up your own role. Write it here.)

Task 2 Now do the role play with some other groups. One member of your group should stay behind to act as a Server, using your restaurant's menu. The other members of your group should act as Customers at other groups' restaurants.

Units 1 & 2

Task

The activities below will help you review and reflect on (think about) what you have learned in **Units 1** and **2**.

1. What useful new words, conversational expressions, or grammar/usage patterns did you learn from the textbook, your teacher, or classmates?

   Example: _appetizer_

2. Write sentences of your own using the new words, conversational expressions, or grammar/usage patterns you wrote above.

   Example: The appetizers on the menu look delicious.

3. What else did you learn in this class about language, culture, etc.?

Unit 3

You, Shopping

Activity I Discuss the Topic

Task *Read and think about the questions below. Make up one question of your own. Write short answers in the spaces, and then discuss the questions in pairs or small groups.*

1. How often do you go shopping? What do you like to shop for?

2. What is your favorite store? Why do you like it?

3. Do you prefer shopping with friends, with a parent, or by yourself? Why?

4. When was the last time you bought something expensive? What was it?

5. When was the last time you got a good deal on something you bought? What was it?

6. Have you ever bought something and later decided you didn't like it? What was wrong with it?

7. Have you ever bargained with a shop owner or clerk to try to get a better price? How did that go?

8. If you had a lot of money, what would you go out and buy right now?

9. Your Question _____

| Activity II | Getting Ready — A Store of Your Own |

Task 1 Pretend that you're going to open a new store of your own. Get together with two or three other students. Decide what kind of store you want to open and what your store's name will be. Write this information below.

Kind of store

_____

Name of your store

_____

Examples of Sales Points

cheap	good quality
useful	beautiful
unique	popular

_____ _____

Task 2 Imagine that you are having a sale in your store. In the boxes below, draw pictures of your top-four sale items. Include the sales points and prices.

Your Sale Items

SALE

Sales Points _____

Price   _____

SALE

Sales Points _____

Price   _____

SALE

Sales Points _____

Price   _____

SALE

Sales Points _____

Price   _____

You, Shopping

Activity III Role Plays — Can I help you with anything?

Task First, practice acting out the role play below with your group from **Activity II**, using the sale items, sales points, and prices you came up with in **Activity II**. Then one student should stay behind and play the role of Sales Clerk, while the others should visit some of the other stores in class and act as Customers. When you finish, come back to your original group and switch roles so everyone gets a chance to play the role of Sales Clerk.

Situation: In a store   **Roles:** Customer   Sales Clerk

Model Conversation

Sales Clerk: Hi. Can I help you with anything?

Customer: Yeah, thanks. I see you're having a sale today.

Sales Clerk: Yes, I'll show you some things we have on sale.
First, we have this ____(item)____ . It's ____(sales points)____ .
Next, we have a ____(item)____ . It's ____(sales points)____ .
Then, we have this ____(item)____ . It's ____(sales points)____ .
Finally, we have these ____(items)____ . They're ____(sales points)____ .

Customer: I like the ____(item)____ .
But do you have it in a larger size?
smaller size?
different color?
different style?
_____?
Could you give me a better price?

Sales Clerk: OK. Let me check.
or
Sorry, that won't be possible.
or
Well, let me talk to my manager.

Unit 3

Activity IV Look What I Bought!

Task In the boxes below, draw pictures of the things you bought in the other stores you visited in **Activity III**. Then talk with your original group members about the things you bought, why you bought them, and how much money you spent on each item.

Items You Bought

Why you bought it _____

Price _____

Why you bought it _____

Price _____

Why you bought it _____

Price _____

Why you bought it _____

Price _____

You, Shopping

Unit 4

You, Out on the Town

Activity I Discuss the Topic

Task *Read and think about the questions below. Make up one question of your own. Write short answers in the spaces, and then discuss the questions in pairs or small groups.*

1. What kinds of things do you like to do when you go out on the town with your friends?

2. Which of the activities below do you like most? Rate them from 1 to 5. Add one activity of your own.

```
       not very fun              very fun
         1    2    3    4    5
```

go to karaoke ____	go shopping ____	go to a movie ____
walk in the park ____	go out to eat ____	go to a museum ____
go to a game center ____	go bowling ____	sit by the river ____
go to Starbucks ____	go for a drive ____	_____ ____

3. Think back to a time when you had an especially good time out on the town with friends. What did you do? Who were you with? What made it so much fun?

4. Have you ever had a bad time out on the town? What happened?

5. Your Question _____

| Activity II | Getting Ready — Where to go? |

| Task 1 | Look at this advertisement for a popular café. Notice the important information it includes: location, opening and closing times, menu, special events, etc. Does it sound like a place you would like to go to? |

Example Advertisement

| Task 2 | Think of a place (café, restaurant, club, pub, etc.) you would like to go to for a day or night out on the town. In the box below, draw an advertisement for the place. Be sure to include all the important information about it, like in the example above. |

Your Advertisement

Activity III Write About it — My Plan for a Good Time

Task In the space below write your own plan for a good time out on the town with some friends. Include details on where and when you and your friends will meet, what transportation you will use, what places you will go to, how much it will cost, and what time you expect to get home.

Useful Language

My friends and I will meet at __(time)__ at __(place)__.
We will get around by __(bus, train, walking, etc.)__.
First, we'll go to __(name of place)__ to __(what you will do there)__.
Then we'll go to __(name of another place)__ to __(what you will do there)__.
We'll need about __(amount of money)__.
We'll probably get home at around __(time)__.

Your Plan

This is my plan for a good time …

Activity IV — Discussion — Your Plan or Mine?

Task: Get together with two or three other students and tell each other about your plans for a good time out on the town. As you listen to the other members talk about their plans, make notes in the boxes. Then discuss which plan sounds like the most fun. You can combine plans to make a really great plan. Write your group's final plan below.

Model Conversation

A: Hi. Do you want to do something this Friday night?
B: Sure. What do you have in mind?
A: Well, how does this sound? First, we'll meet at …. (Tell your plan from **Activity III**.)
B: That sounds like fun. I have a plan, too. Do you want to hear it?
A: Sure.
B: First, we'll meet at ….

Your Group Members' Plans

Plan 1

Plan 2

Plan 3

Final Group Plan

Units 3 & 4

> **Task**
>
> The activities below will help you review and reflect on (think about) what you have learned in **Units 3** and **4**.

1. What useful new words, conversational expressions, or grammar/usage patterns did you learn from the textbook, your teacher, or your classmates?

   _____ _____ _____ _____

   _____ _____ _____ _____

   _____ _____ _____ _____

   _____ _____ _____ _____

   _____ _____ _____ _____

   _____ _____ _____ _____

2. Write sentences of your own using the new words, conversational expressions, or grammar/usage patterns you wrote above.

   _____

   _____

   _____

   _____

   _____

   _____

3. What else did you learn in this class about language, culture, etc.?

Unit 5

You, Planning a Trip

Activity 1   Discuss the Topic

Task *Read and think about the questions below. Make up one question of your own. Write short answers in the spaces, and then discuss the questions in pairs or small groups.*

1. What trips have you taken in Japan or abroad? Where did you go? How was it?

2. For your next trip, would you prefer to travel in Japan or abroad? Where would you like to go?

3. Have you ever gotten help from a travel agency for a trip? Did they just sell you a ticket, or did they give you travel advice or recommend a tour for you?

4. Would you ever like to go on an organized package tour? What are the advantages and disadvantages of joining such a tour?

5. Would you like to work in a travel agency someday? Why or why not?

6. When you travel, what do you prefer – shopping, outdoor activities, sightseeing, restaurants, or nightlife?

7. What place would you recommend for someone who wants to take a trip in Japan? How about a trip abroad? Why?

8. Your Question _____

Activity II Getting Ready — The Perfect Tour

Task 1 *Get together with two or three other students. Pretend you all work in a travel agency, and your boss has asked you to create a new tour that university students would be interested in taking during their next vacation. The tour can either be in Japan or abroad and should last between 6-9 days. First, give your travel agency a name. Then write your tour details below.*

Your travel agency's name: _____

Tour Details

1. Where the tour will go (destination)
   _____

2. When the tour will take place (exact dates)
   _____

3. How tour members will travel to and from the destination (transportation)
   _____

4. Where they will stay (accommodation)
   _____

5. What they will see and do (activities and places of interest)
   _____

6. How much the tour will cost (total cost)
   _____

7. Other important information (meals, optional tours, special events)
   _____

Task 2 *Look at the sample tour advertisement below. Notice what information is included.*

Example Tour Advertisement

Thailand Phuket

TOTAL PRICE – ¥79,000 INCLUDES:

Roundtrip airfare on Thai Airways
Six nights at Peaceful Beach Bungalows
Delicious Breakfast Buffet included
Option: scuba diving, snorkeling, and 18-hole golf course nearby

Unit 5

Task 3 — In the box below create an advertisement for the tour you created in Task 1. Make sure you include all the important information. Add a drawing to make your ad more interesting.

Your Tour Advertisement

Activity III — Write About it — Your Tour Plan

Task — Write a detailed plan for your tour. Include all the information you wrote in **Activity II** as well as anything else you think is important.

Your Tour Plan

This tour will go to…

Activity IV Role Play — Your Fantastic Tour!

Task 1 *First, practice the role play below with your group members, using the information from the tour you created in **Activity II**. Then one student should stay behind and play the role of Travel Agent, while the others should visit some of the other travel agencies in class and act as Customers. When you finish, come back to your original group and switch roles so everyone gets a chance to be the Travel Agent.*

Situation: At a travel agency **Roles:** Travel Agent Customer

Model Conversation

Travel Agent: Welcome. Please, have a seat. How can I help you?

Customer: Thanks. Do you have any interesting tours planned for the next school vacation?

Travel Agent: Yes, we have a fantastic tour to ____(tour destination)____.

Customer: Oh, really? Could you tell me more?

Travel Agent: Sure. ____(explain tour while showing advertisement)____.

Customer: I have a few questions. First, _____?
And, _____?
Also, _____?

Travel Agent: ____(answers questions)____.

Customer: Thanks for the information. I'll think about it.

Task 2 *Join your original group and discuss the different tours you heard about in other "travel agencies." Decide which tours you want to go on the most. List them below.*

Most Interesting Tours

First Choice _____

Second Choice _____

Third Choice _____

Unit 6

You, Hotel Guest

Activity I Discuss the Topic

Task *Read and think about the questions below. Make up one question of your own. Write short answers in the spaces, and then discuss the questions in pairs or small groups.*

1. What hotel, ryokan, or minshuku have you stayed in? What was it like?

2. What are some differences between staying in a hotel, ryokan, and minshuku? What are the advantages and disadvantages of staying in each place?

3. What are some problems that can happen when you stay in a hotel, ryokan, or minshuku?

4. When you make a reservation, what are some of the things you can ask for in a hotel, ryokan, or minshuku to make your stay nicer?

5. When traveling abroad, people sometimes stay in a youth hostel. Youth hostels are an inexpensive dormitory-style place with many beds in one room. Have you ever stayed in a youth hostel? Would you like to try one? Why or why not?

6. Have you ever reserved a room with Airbnb and then stayed in someone's house? How was it? If not, would you like to try an Airbnb? Why or why not?

7. Your Question _____

| Activity II | Getting Ready — Making a Reservation |

Task 1 Read this hotel information sheet. Then fill in the Online Reservation form.

SAN FRANCISCO BAYVIEW HOTEL

14 Market Street
San Francisco, California
1- 415-555-2323

Free Wifi   Swimming Pool
Exercise Club   Restaurant and Rooftop Bar

Airport pick-up and drop-off possible – *$25*
Breakfast Buffet – *$10*

36-inch LCD-screen TV
Smoking/Non-smoking rooms

Room Prices: Single room – *$100*
Double room – *$125*
(king-size bed or two twin beds)
Family room (with rollaway bed) – *$140*
1 bedroom suite – *$200*

Online Reservation Form

Your Name	
Email Address	
Telephone #	
Check-in date	Check-out date
How many nights?	
Type of room	Single room ☐ Double room (king) ☐ Double room (twin) ☐ Suite ☐ Extra Rollaway bed ☐ Smoking ☐ Non-Smoking ☐
Breakfast buffet?	yes ☐ no ☐
Airport pick-up?	yes ☐ no ☐
Airport drop-off?	yes ☐ no ☐
How will you pay?	Visa ☐ Mastercard ☐ American Express ☐ Discover ☐
Credit Card #	Expiration date Security code
Special requests?	

Task 2 With a partner, practice this **Model Conversation** using the Hotel Information Sheet in *Activity II*.

Model Conversation

Front Desk: Hello, San Francisco Bayview Hotel. How can I help you?
Guest: Hi. I'd like to make a reservation.
Front Desk: One moment, please. OK. What day will you arrive?
Guest: I'll arrive on August 10th and check out on the morning of August 13th.
Front Desk: OK. That's three nights. How many rooms will you need?
Guest: Just one room for two, please.
Front Desk: Would you like a king size bed or two twin beds?
Guest: I'd like a king size bed, please. And I'd like to request a quiet room with a nice view, if possible.
Front Desk: OK. That will depend on what's available when you check in, but I will make a note of your request, and we will do the best we can. The price for three nights will be $375.00 plus tax. I can reserve the room for you now if you give me your name and your credit card number.
Guest: OK ... My name is Bill Jones. Here is the credit card number and expiration date.
Front Desk: OK. Your room is reserved, Mr. Jones. We will see you on August 10.

Task 3 Get together with two other students. Pretend that you will open a new hotel. Think of a name for your hotel, and then make your own hotel information sheet in the box below. Using the hotel information sheet in **Task 1** as a model. Then practice the conversation in Task 2 again, using information about your new hotel.

Hotel Information Sheet

_____
(hotel name)

Activity III   Role Plays — At the Hotel

Task *Practice the role play situations below with your group members. Add a problem of your own for each situation. After you have all taken turns playing both the Guest and Front Desk Clerk roles, one student should stay behind and act as the Front Desk Clerk for new Guests from other groups. The other members of your group should become Guests in the other hotels in class.*

1. Situation: Checking in at a hotel (face to face)   **Roles:** Guest   Front Desk Clerk

Model Conversation

Front Desk: Hello. Welcome to ___(hotel name)___ . How can I help you?
Guest: Hi. My name is Kenji Ito. I have a reservation for tonight.
Front Desk: OK. Here's your key. You're in Room 523.
Guest: Thanks. Could you tell me about the room?
Front Desk: Yes, it's a nice room but ___(describe problem)___ .
Guest: 1) That's all right. We're really tired.
2) Well, that's not going to work for us. ___(explain and negotiate)___ .
3) Can I speak with the manager, please? ___(negotiate)___ .

Problems
1. You want a king size bed, but they only have a room with two twin beds.
2. You want a room with a good ocean view, not a view of the building next door.
3. You want a non-smoking room, but they don't have any available.
4. The room is still being cleaned, and you will have to wait.
5. _____

2. Situation: Calling from the room (phone conversation)   **Roles:** Guest   Front Desk Clerk

Model Conversation

Front Desk: Hello, Front Desk.
Guest: Hi. I'm in Room 523. ___(explain problem or request)___ .
Front Desk: Sure, I can help with that. ___(give possible solutions)___ .

Problem Request
1. This non-smoking room smells smoky.
2. There are noisy people in the hall.
3. The TV doesn't work.
4. You can't connect to the wifi.
5. You ordered food from Room Service, but it hasn't arrived yet.
6. You want a late check out tomorrow at 6 pm.
7. You want information on local tourist places.
8. _____

3. Situation: Checking out (face to face)

Roles: Guest   Front Desk Clerk

Model Conversation

Guest: I'd like to check out now.
Clerk: May I have your key, please? What's your name?
Guest: It's Ito. Kenji Ito.
Clerk: Did you have anything from the mini-bar?
Guest: No, we didn't have anything.
Clerk: OK. Here's your receipt. Thanks for staying with us.
Guest: Excuse me.   (explain problem/request) .

Problems/Request

1. The hotel made a mistake with the mini-bar charges.
2. They forgot to give you back the deposit.
3. You want to make a reservation for a future stay.
4. You need a taxi to the airport.
5. _____

4. Situation: After checking out (phone conversation)

Roles: Guest   Front Desk Clerk

Model Conversation (on the phone)

Front Desk: Hello,   (hotel name) .
Guest: Hi. I stayed in your hotel last night and   (explain problems) .
Front Desk: Do you remember the room number?
Guest: Yes, I was in Room 523.
Front Desk: OK. Let me check with Housekeeping.
  Yes, we have it here. Will you come pick it up, or should we send it to you?
       or
  I'm sorry, but we didn't find anything in your room after you left.

Problems

1. You forgot a jacket in the closet.
2. You forgot your passport in the safe.
3. You can't find your cell phone.
4. You forgot your phone charger in the wall socket.
5. _____

Review and Reflection

Units 5 & 6

Task

*The activities below will help you review and reflect on (think about) what you have learned in **Units 5** and **6**.*

1. What useful new words, conversational expressions, or grammar/usage patterns did you learn from the textbook, your teacher, or your classmates?

   _____   _____   _____   _____

   _____   _____   _____   _____

   _____   _____   _____   _____

   _____   _____   _____   _____

   _____   _____   _____   _____

2. Write sentences of your own using the new words, conversational expressions, or grammar/usage patterns you wrote above.

   _____

   _____

   _____

   _____

   _____

   _____

   _____

3. What else did you learn in this class about language, culture, etc.?

Unit 7

You, World Traveler

Activity 1 — Discuss the Topic

Task *Read and think about the questions below. Make up one question of your own. Write short answers in the spaces, and then discuss the questions in pairs or small groups.*

1. If sometime soon you could go on a trip abroad to any country you wanted, where would you go? Why?

2. What things do you have to do to get ready to go on a trip abroad?

3. Before you go on a trip, do you make up a list of things to do and take with you, or do you leave everything to the last minute?

4. Which do you prefer, traveling alone, with a friend or family member, or in a group? Why?

5. What are some problems that can come up when people travel abroad?

6. On a trip abroad, what do you hope to learn or experience?

7. Your Question _____

Activity II — Getting Ready — Planning a Trip Abroad

Task 1 *Pretend that you are planning a trip abroad. First, decide where and when you will go. Write the place you will go to and the month you will travel below. Then write your ideas in the three "to do" lists below.*

Destination: What country will you go to? _____

Departure date: What month will you go? _____

Travel "To Do" Lists

Things to do before you go	Things to take on your trip	Things you want to do on your trip

Task 2 *Now get together with two or three other students and tell about your lists. If the other members come up with any ideas that you like, add them to your lists.*

Useful Language

Talking about your trip

I'm going to ____(place)____ in ____(month)____.

Before I go, I'll _____.

I'll be sure to take _____.

On my trip I want to _____.

Activity III Role Plays — Travel Problems

Task In small groups, act out the four travel situations below. Take turns playing the different roles in each situation and for each problem. Make up one problem of your own for each situation. Before you begin the role play, discuss what problems you will act out.

1. **Situation:** At the check-in counter at the airport
   Roles: Ticket Agent   Passenger   Supervisor

1. Passenger's passport has expired.
2. Passenger is late getting to the airport.
3. Passenger's bags are too heavy.
4. Flight is canceled until tomorrow.
5. Passenger wants an aisle seat.
6. Passenger does not have the proper visa.
7. Passenger wants to take a pet on the plane.
8. Your problem

_____

Useful Language

May I see your ticket and passport, please?

I'm sorry, but I have some bad news.

Can I speak to your supervisor, please?

2. **Situation:** On the plane
   Roles: Flight Attendant   Passenger   Supervisor

Problems

1. Passenger doesn't like the food.
2. Passenger feels sick.
3. Passenger has had too much to drink.
4. Passenger smokes in the bathroom.
5. Passenger wants a date with the flight attendant.
6. Your problem

_____

Useful Language

Excuse me?
Yes, may I help you?
I have a problem.

3. **Situation:** At the immigration counter

   Roles: Immigration Officer   Traveler   Supervisor

Problems

1. Traveler left his/her passport on the plane.
2. Traveler cannot speak English.
3. Traveler is a suspected terrorist.
4. Traveler looks like a criminal or gang member.
5. Traveler has a tourist visa but has almost no money (probably coming to work, not as a tourist).
6. Your problem _____

Useful Language  18

May I see your passport and arrival card, please?
What is the purpose of your visit?
Excuse me, but I'm going to call my supervisor.

4. **Situation:** At the customs counter

   Roles: Customs Officer   Traveler   Supervisor

Problems

1. Traveler is carrying fresh fruits and vegetables.
2. Traveler is carrying a fake Louis Vuitton bag.
3. Traveler has illegal drugs in his/her bag.
4. Traveler has a gun in his/her bag.
5. Traveler has a lot of cash (more than 1,000,000 yen).
6. Traveler has a bottle of vitamins with no label on it, so it looks like illegal drugs
7. Your problem _____

Useful Language   19

May I see your passport and customs declaration form, please?
Do you have anything to declare?
Would you open this bag, please?
Did you know it's illegal to bring this into this country?
Excuse me, but I'm going to call my supervisor.

Unit 8

You, Living with Others

Activity I   Discuss the Topic

Task *Read and think about the questions below. Make up one question of your own. Write short answers in the spaces, and then discuss the questions in pairs or small groups.*

1. What experiences have you had living with people? What are the good things about living with people? What problems can come up when you live with family, friends, or strangers?

2. Have you ever lived alone? What are the good things about living alone? What are the difficult things?

3. Do you think you are an easy person to live with? Why or Why not?

4. Have you ever done a homestay abroad or lived in a dormitory? If so, how did that go? If not, do you think it would be fun to do so? Why? Why not?

5. Have you ever shared a room/apartment with someone? How was that? What problems were there, if any?

6. Have you ever had a problem with someone or a complaint and decided to talk to the person about it? What did the person say or do?

7. Has anyone ever complained to you about something that you did? Did you apologize, give an explanation or find a solution together?

8. Your Question _____

Activity II Homestay/Dormitory Personality Questionnaire

Task 1 *Pretend that you are going abroad and will be sharing a room in a dormitory or homestay. To find a good roommate, you may need to answer a personality questionnaire. Circle the place on each line that best describes you.*

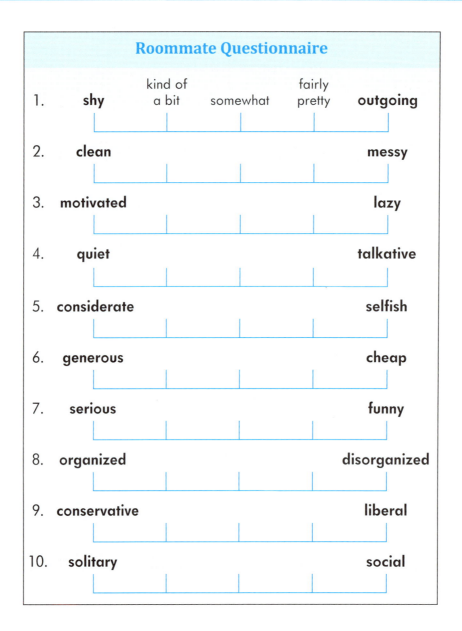

Task 2 *Join a group and tell about yourself. Which group member are you most like? What three qualities would you most want a roommate to have? Write them below.*

1. _____ 2. _____ 3. _____

Activity III Role Plays — Problems with Roommates

Task: With a partner, read through the list of Problems/Complaints below. Add one idea of your own. Then take the role of Student (you) or Roommate and work to solve the different problems/complaints. Make sure you switch roles for each problem/complaint.

Situation: Solving problems with a roommate

Roles: Student   Your Roommate

Model Conversation

Student: Hi. Do you have a minute?
Roommate: Sure. What's up?
Student: I hope you don't mind my saying this, but ___(describe the problem)___. ←**Problem/Complaint**
Roommate: Sorry about that. ←**Apology**
                   But ___(explain)_____. ←**Explanation**
                   OK. From now on I will _____. ←**Solution**
                   OK. From now on let's _____. ←**Solution**

Problems/Complaints

1. Your roommate likes to listen to music while studying, but you like quiet.

2. Your roommate often comes back late at night and wakes you up.

3. Your roommate often leaves food in the refrigerator for a long time, and it smells bad.

4. There is a no-smoking rule in your room, but sometimes when you come back to your room, it smells like smoke.

5. You want to have some private time with your girlfriend or boyfriend, but your roommate is always in the room.

6. Your room is very messy and you want your roommate to clean it up.

7. Your food disappears from the refrigerator sometimes, and you want to know why.

8. _____

Activity IV — Homestay Questionnaire

Task: In order to match you with a good homestay you often have to fill out a questionnaire asking about your wants and needs. Answer the questions below and then get together with some classmates and compare your answers.

Homestay Questionnaire

1. Do you have any allergies to foods, cats, medicine, etc.?

2. Are there any foods you don't like to eat?

3. Are there any foods that you must have in the house?

4. Do you like children? What age children would you prefer to live with?

5. Do you smoke? If not, could you live in a house with smokers?

6. Do you drink alcohol? Do you mind living with someone who drinks?

7. Do you need a house with a bathtub, or is just a shower OK?

8. Do you like to spend a lot of time alone, or do you prefer to spend time with other people, chatting, watching TV together, etc.?

Activity V — Role Plays — Solving Problems at a Homestay

Task: With a partner, read through the Problems/Complaints below. Add one idea of your own. Then take the role of Student or Homestay Parent and work to find a solution for the different problems/complaints. Make sure you switch roles for each problem/complaint.

Situation: Solving problems at a homestay

Roles: Student   Homestay Parent

Model Conversation

Student: I'm sorry to bother you, but can we talk?
Homestay parent: Sure. What's on your mind?
Student: Well, I have a problem. _____. ←Problem/Complaint
  or
  Well, I hope you don't mind me saying this, but it bothers me that _____. ←Problem/Complaint
Homestay parent: Thanks for telling me. I'm sorry to hear that.
  Let's do this. _____. ←Solution
  How about if we do this? _____. ←Solution
  What do you think of this idea? _____. ←Solution
  What is your idea?
Student: OK. Thanks for your help. Let's _____. ←Solution

Problems/Complaints

1. You have a bad cold and want to go to a doctor.
2. The children in the house are noisy early in the morning and keep waking you up.
3. You don't know how to get to the school from the house.
4. The food doesn't taste good or there is not enough food or too much food to eat.
5. It's very difficult for you to understand your homestay parent's English.
6. There is a 10 p.m. curfew in the house, but you sometimes want to come back later.
7. Your homestay brother or sister smokes, and it bothers you.
8. You want to stay overnight at a friend's house.
9. You have a problem with a teacher or another student at school.
10. (Your idea) _____

Units 7 & 8

Task

*The activities below will help you review and reflect on (think about) what you have learned in **Units 7** and **8**.*

1. What useful new words, conversational expressions, or grammar/usage patterns did you learn from the textbook, your teacher, or your classmates?

   _____ _____ _____ _____

   _____ _____ _____ _____

   _____ _____ _____ _____

   _____ _____ _____ _____

   _____ _____ _____ _____

   _____ _____ _____ _____

2. Write sentences of your own using the new words, conversational expressions, or grammar/usage patterns you wrote above.

   _____

   _____

   _____

   _____

   _____

   _____

   _____

3. What else did you learn in this class about language, culture, etc.?

Unit 9: You, Job Hunting

Activity I Discuss the Topic

Task *Read and think about the questions below. Make up one question of your own. Write short answers in the spaces, and then discuss the questions in pairs or small groups.*

1. Do you have a part-time job now? What is it? Do you like it? If not, did you have a part-time job before?

2. When you were a child, what work did you want to do when you grew up?

3. What is your "dream job" for the future?

4. What kind of work do you think you would **not** be good at? Why?

5. Have you ever had a bad or difficult job? What was it? Did you quit?

6. People work to make money, of course, but they also have other reasons for working. What are some of those reasons?

7. If you were a boss, what would be an important question you would ask a job seeker in an interview?

8. Your Question _____

Activity II — Getting Ready — You, Company Manager

Task 1 Get together with two or three other students. Pretend that you are the managers of a company and in charge of hiring a new employee. Decide what kind of company you work for, your company's name, and the job you will be hiring the person to do.

What kind of company? _____

Name of your company? _____

What job? _____

Task 2 Read through the list of personal qualities in the box below. Add two more qualities of your own. As managers, circle the five qualities that you think are the most important in the person you will hire for the job.

Personal Qualities

friendly	careful	hard-working	experienced
creative	energetic	stylish	independent
cooperative	intelligent	punctual	fun to work with
easy-going	a "good talker"	physically strong	imaginative
"computer savvy"	dependable	_____	_____

Activity III — Getting Ready — You, Company Manager

Task Next, you will do interviews to find a good employee for the job you decided on in **Activity II**. What questions would you ask the job seekers? Write your questions below.

1. _____
2. _____
3. _____
4. _____
5. _____

Activity IV — Getting Ready — Your Strong Points

Task: During a job interview you should always look for chances to talk about your strong points (without overdoing it, of course). What do you think are your best qualities? Write them below. Give details and examples. Refer to **Activity II** for the qualities employers might be looking for in an employee.

My Strong Points

1. I am … _____
2. I can … _____
3. _____
4. _____

Activity V — Role Play 1 — A Job Interview

Task 1: In this role play, a Job Seeker has an interview for the job at the company that you wrote about in **Activity II**. Practice the role play, taking turns playing the roles of Interviewer and Job Seeker. Then two group members should visit other companies in class to be interviewed for the jobs they are hiring for. Two members should stay behind and play the role of Interviewers at your company. Switch roles so that you all get to play both Interviewer and Job Seeker roles.

Situation: Job Interview   **Roles:** Job Seeker   Interviewer (Manager)

Model Conversation 22

Interviewer: Come in. Please have a seat. First, let me tell you about our company. ____(company name)____ is a ____(type of company)____ that ____(makes/does)____. Now, I'd like to ask you some questions. (Interviewer asks questions from **Activity III**.)

Job Seeker: (answers Interviewer's questions)

Interviewer: Do you have any questions about this job?

Job Seeker: (asks questions about the job)

Interviewer: (answers questions) Thanks for coming in today. We'll contact you soon.

Task 2 *First, write notes about the companies and jobs you were interviewed for as a Job Seeker. Then write notes about the people you interviewed as an Interviewer.*

Job Seeker's Notes

	Company	Job	Interesting Information
1.	_____	_____	_____
2.	_____	_____	_____
3.	_____	_____	_____
4.	_____	_____	_____

Interviewer's Notes

	Name	Interesting Information	Strong Points
1.	_____	_____	_____
2.	_____	_____	_____
3.	_____	_____	_____
4.	_____	_____	_____

Activity VI — Role Play 2 — Fun Roles

Task 1 *Do this role play with your original group first, then visit other companies as you did in **Activity V**. This time choose a role from the Job Seeker Roles and Interviewer Roles lists below. Don't tell the others what your role is. Use the language, facial expressions, and body language that match the role. (Before beginning the role play, Interviewers should think up new interview questions that match their role.) After each role play, try to guess what roles the other group members were playing and then discuss this together.*

Job Seeker Roles

1. You are lazy. No hard work for you.
2. Money is all you think about.
3. You are in a Punk Rock band and are too busy to work overtime or on the weekend.
4. You want this job so badly that you will tell lies to get it.
5. You are very proud of your education and family background.
6. You are nervous and lack self-confidence.
7. You are very competitive and try to look better than other applicants.

Interviewer Roles

1. You are bored with interviewing people all day long.
2. You don't really like young people. They all seem lazy.
3. You are very bossy.
4. You are very proud of your company.
5. Your company needs employees to work long overtime hours.
6. It's obvious that you prefer employees of a particular gender – male or female.
7. You ask a lot of questions that don't make sense in this situation.

Task 2 *Write notes below about the jobs you interview for and the job seekers you interview.*

Job Seeker's Notes

	Company	Job	Interesting Information
1.	_____	_____	_____
2.	_____	_____	_____
3.	_____	_____	_____
4.	_____	_____	_____

Interviewer's Notes

	Name	Interesting Information	Strong Points
1.	_____	_____	_____
2.	_____	_____	_____
3.	_____	_____	_____
4.	_____	_____	_____

Unit 10

You, Giving Good Advice

Activity I   Discuss the Topic

Task   *Read and think about the questions below. Make up one question of your own. Write short answers in the spaces, and then discuss the questions in pairs or small groups.*

1. Has anyone ever given you any good advice? What was the advice? Who gave it to you? Was it helpful?

2. Has anyone ever asked you for advice? What was the problem? What advice did you give?

3. Do any of your friends have personal problems right now? (No names, please!) If so, what are the problems?

4. Who do you talk to when you have a problem? Family? Friends? Adults you know? Or do you keep it to yourself?

5. There is an old Italian proverb – "You should only give advice when you are asked for it." Do you agree? Disagree? Why?

6. Your Question _____

Activity II Getting Ready — Patterns for Giving Advice

Task *Here are some sentence patterns you can use when giving advice. Practice saying these examples with a partner and remember that your tone of voice – the way you speak – can make your advice sound more friendly, formal, or urgent, depending on the situation.*

Formal **Authoritative** **Urgent**	**You had better (not) + (verb base form)** Examples: You'd better be more careful. You'd better not do that again.
	You ought to + (verb base form) Examples: You ought to quit smoking. You ought to eat more vegetables.
Standard Form	**You should (not) + (verb base form)** Examples: You should take a vacation. You shouldn't talk to him.
Friendly **Informal**	**If I were you I would (not) + (verb base form)** Examples: If I were you, I would relax today. If I were you, I wouldn't eat that.
	Why don't you + (verb base form)? Examples: Why don't you take a taxi? Why don't you quit that job?
	How about (not) + (verb + ing) Examples: How about getting more exercise? How about not going out tonight?

Activity III Write About it — Advice Column: "Dear Hana"

Task Read the personal problems below. Pretend you are Hana—an advice columnist for a newspaper—and give each person some good advice. Write your advice in the spaces below. The expression "I think you should ..." is probably the most common way to give advice. But for this activity, try to use some of the other patterns for giving advice presented in **Activity II**.

Problem 1 - Ken

Dear Hana:

I really need your advice. My sister is 25 years old, and she is planning to get married in a few months. All the plans are set, and our two families have met for dinner and gotten to know each other. My sister's fiancé seems like a nice guy, but last week I was at a restaurant with some friends, and I looked out the window and saw my sister's fiancé walk by with another girl. They both looked very happy, and she was holding his arm really tight. He didn't see me, but now I'm worried that this was his girlfriend. I really don't know what to do. What's your advice?

_____
_____
_____
_____

Problem 2 - Junko

Dear Hana:

I live in an apartment house that has a lot of students. I was happy there for a year, but recently a guy moved in to the apartment next to mine. The problem is this guy is really noisy. He sometimes plays his music until 3 or 4 a.m. His friends come over and they party until the early hours of the morning. I can't sleep with all the noise. In this apartment house we have a rule to be quiet between 10 p.m. and 8 a.m., and I have spoken to him about it. He always apologizes and says he understands, but after a few days he starts being noisy again. I'm sick of it! I talked to the apartment manager a couple of times, but she's the guy's aunt. She says she will talk to him, but nothing ever changes. Do you have any advice for me?

_____
_____
_____
_____

Problem 3 - Takashi

Dear Hana:

I have a difficult problem. I really like my best friend's ex-girlfriend, Mika. I can tell she likes me too, but I think my friend is still in love with her. They broke up more than a year ago, but he still seems to hope they can get back together. I'm worried that if I date this girl, he will be hurt and angry with me. It could ruin our friendship. We have been friends for more than 10 years now. But Mika is really cool, and I think we would be a really great couple. The situation seems unfair. What should I do? Can you give me some good advice?

_____
_____
_____
_____

Problem 4 - Eri

Dear Hana:

Here's my problem. I'm a fourth-year university student. Last year I did a homestay in New Zealand where I met a guy, Michael. We got along really well, and did a lot of fun things together. After I came back to Japan, we started talking on Skype about getting married or living together after I graduate. Anyway, Michael decided to come over and live here for a while. But since he got here, it's been really difficult. He seems very different from when we were in New Zealand. At first it was great to have him here in Japan, but he wants to spend all his free time with me. He found a job teaching English to kids, but he doesn't like it very much. He always complains about the food, and he's made very little effort to learn Japanese. To tell the truth, I'm getting fed up with him. I don't know what to do. Please help!

_____
_____
_____
_____

Activity IV Discussion — Good Advice!

Task: *Get together with two or three other students and discuss what advice you would give the people in **Activity III**. Then, in the spaces below, write the best advice you heard from your group members.*

Problem 1 – Ken

_____

_____

Problem 2 – Junko

_____

_____

Problem 3 – Takashi

_____

_____

Problem 4 – Eri

_____

_____

Activity V Write About it — A Problem to Solve

Task: *Think of a problem a friend or family member has now or had in the past. You can also use a problem of your own, or an imaginary problem. Write about the problem in detail below.*

_____

_____

_____

_____

_____

Activity VI Write About it — A Friend Has a Problem

Task *Tell your class members about the problem you wrote about in **Activity V**. Ask for advice and write the advice you get below. Listen to your classmates' problems and give them some good advice, too. Write down their problems and your advice. Again, use as many of the patterns for giving advice from **Activity II** as possible.*

Model Conversation

A: Hi, how's it going?
B: Well, my friend has a problem.
A: Oh, really? What's the problem?
B: ____(describe problem)____. What do you think he/she should do?
A: ____(give advice)____.
B: Thanks for the advice!

Your Classmates' Advice to You

1. _____
2. _____
3. _____
4. _____
5. _____
6. _____

Your Classmates' Problems	Your Advice
1. _____	_____
2. _____	_____
3. _____	_____
4. _____	_____
5. _____	_____
6. _____	_____

You, Giving Good Advice

Review and Reflection

Units 9 & 10

> **Task**
>
> The activities below will help you review and reflect on (think about) what you have learned in **Units 9** and **10**.

1. What useful new words, conversational expressions, or grammar/usage patterns did you learn from the textbook, your teacher, or your classmates?

   _____ _____ _____ _____

   _____ _____ _____ _____

   _____ _____ _____ _____

   _____ _____ _____ _____

   _____ _____ _____ _____

   _____ _____ _____ _____

2. Write sentences of your own using the new words, conversational expressions, or grammar/usage patterns you wrote above.

   _____

   _____

   _____

   _____

   _____

   _____

3. What else did you learn in this class about language, culture, etc.?

Unit 11

You, Solving World Problems

Activity 1 Discuss the Topic

Task *Read and think about the questions below. Make up one question of your own. Write short answers in the spaces, and then discuss the questions in pairs or small groups.*

1. Think about which of the problems below are the most serious problems in the world today. Add two problems of your own. Choose the five most serious problems and rank them in order of seriousness from 1 to 5, with 1 being the most serious. (Write your rank numbers on the lines.)

   crime _____ HIV/AIDs _____ poverty _____ pollution _____ nuclear weapons _____
   drug abuse _____ unemployment _____ overpopulation _____ illiteracy _____
   endangered species _____ racial discrimination _____ gender discrimination _____
   terrorism _____ environmental destruction _____ global warming _____ war _____
   _____ _____ _____ _____

2. Look at the world problem that you ranked as the most serious. (#1) Why is this such a serious problem?

3. What is being done to help solve these world problems? What NGOs, NPOs, or charity organizations are working to solve them? (for example: Save the Children or World Wildlife Fund (WWF))

4. How do these NGOs, NPOs, and charities raise money to do their work?

5. Have you ever done volunteer work or donated money to an NGO, NPO, or charity? What did you do to help?

6. Your Question _____

Activity II Getting Ready — A Serious World Problem

Task 1 Look back at the world problems you discussed in **Activity I**. Get together with two or three other students and decide which world problem you all would like to learn more about. Use the **Model Conversation** to help you choose the problem you will study.

Model Conversation

Jun: I think ___(world problem)___ is a very serious world problem because _____.

Masako: I agree that problem is serious but I think ___(world problem)___ is an even more serious problem because _____.

Jun: Hmmmm. I see what you mean. What do you think, Kenji?

Kenji: I think ___(world problem)___ is really important. I'd like to learn more about it.

Jun: Good idea. OK, I say we work on Kenji's problem.

What problem will your group learn more about? _____

Task 2 Use your smartphone or a computer to do research on the world problem you chose to learn more about. In the space below, write some reasons why this problem is serious. <u>Be sure to support your argument with facts and data!</u> Later, you will use this information to convince your classmates that this problem is serious.

Research Tip – To start your search, type the name of the world problem in the search box at either Google.com or Wikipedia.org.

Why is this problem serious?

_____
_____
_____
_____
_____

Facts and data

_____
_____

Activity III — Getting Ready — Working to Solve the Problem

Task: *Use your smartphone or a computer to do research to find an NGO, NPO, or charity that is working to solve the problem you chose in **Activity II**. Write the name of this NGO, NPO, or charity in the space and then explain what they are doing to solve this world problem.*

Research Tip – Type the name of the world problem followed by the words charity, NPO, or NGO in the search box at these websites:

google.com   idealist.org   guidestar.org

charitiesdirect.com   charity.co.jp

Your NGO, NPO, or charity's name _____

What is your NGO, NPO, or charity doing to solve the problem?

_____
_____
_____
_____
_____
_____

Activity IV — Role Play — Raising Money to Donate

Task 1: *Pretend you work for the NGO, NPO, or charity you wrote about in **Activity III**. Get together with two or three other students and give them a short presentation to convince them that they should support your NGO, NPO, or charity. Explain the world problem and what your NGO, NPO, or charity is doing to solve it. Ask them to donate money to your NGO, NPO, or charity. Take turns being the NGO, NPO, or Charity Worker. Use the **Useful Language** on the next page as a guide.*

Situation: NGO, NPO, or Charity Worker is looking for people to donate money to his group.

Roles: NGO, NPO, or Charity Worker

Donor (with 10,000 yen to spend)

Useful Language

NGO, NPO, or Charity Worker Presentation

Step 1 – Explain the problem
Hi. We think illiteracy is a really serious problem because it's very hard to find a good job if you can't read or write, especially if you live in a city. Without a good job, it's difficult to earn enough money to feed your family and get good medical care. Here is an important fact: Did you know that in 2018, only 64% of the people in Nepal can read? Among women, only 53% can read. This is a big problem.

Step 2 – Explain what your NGO, NPO, or charity is doing to solve the problem
I work for an NPO called ETC — Educate the Children. We raise money to help children in Nepal stay in school so they can learn to read and write. We also help women in the villages learn to do various kinds of work so they can have a better life.

Step 3 – Ask for a donation
I hope you can donate some money to our NPO.

Teacher talks to children, Kanchenjunga Trek, Nepal - circa May 2012. ©Michal Knitl/shutterstock

Task 2 — Make notes about the world problems and the NGOs, NPOs, or charities that your classmates tell you about. Then return to your original group and discuss what you have heard. Your group will have 10,000 yen, and you must decide which NGO, NPO, or charity you will donate this money to.

1. **Classmate's World Problem** _____

   Why is it serious?

   _____

   _____

   Facts _____

   What is the NGO, NPO, or charity doing to solve the problem?

   _____

   _____

2. **Classmate's World Problem** _____

   Why is it serious?

   _____

   _____

   Facts _____

   What is the NGO, NPO, or charity doing to solve the problem?

   _____

   _____

3. **Classmate's World Problem** _____

   Why is it serious?

   _____

   _____

   Facts _____

   What is the NGO, NPO, or charity doing to solve the problem?

   _____

   _____

Which group will you donate your 10,000 yen to? _____

Unit 12
You, Inventor for the Future

Activity 1 Discuss the Topic

Task Read and think about the questions below. Make up one question of your own. Write short answers in the spaces, and then discuss the questions in pairs or small groups.

1. Will life on Earth for humans be better or worse 20 years from now? Why do you think so?

2. What do you imagine your personal life will be like 20 years from now? Where will you be living? Will you be working? Who will you be living with?

3. What is your dream for the future? What big goals do you have for work, travel, etc.?

4. What scares you the most about the future? What are you afraid might happen?

5. Do you think today's "things" – the tools, devices, and appliances like the car, the television, and the smartphone – will still be used 20 years from now? If so, what will they look like?

6. Your Question _____

Activity II — Getting Ready — Things of the Future

Task Think about the world 20 years from now and how life will be different in each category below. What new tools, appliances, and other devices that we don't have now will be used in the future? Write your ideas for each category on the lines below.

Example — Transportation – *Cars will fly.*

Transportation _____

Homes _____

Food and Drink _____

Fashion _____

Education _____

Crime _____

Health _____

Love and Romance _____

Language Learning _____

You, Inventor for the Future

Activity III — Getting Ready – Your Cool Invention for the Future

Task: *Pretend that you are an inventor and that you want to invent a thing, tool or appliance that will be useful 20 years from now. Choose one of your ideas from **Activity II**, or just use your imagination to make up something completely new – even if it sounds "crazy" or "silly." Describe your invention below, and then draw a picture of it in the box.*

Your Invention's name _____

What is it used for? _____

What does it look like? _____

Advantages of using it? _____

Other Information _____

Your Cool Invention for the Future

Activity IV Role Play — Selling your Cool Invention

Task: Get together with a partner. In this role play, Inventors talk with Investors and try to convince them to invest money in their invention. Inventors should describe their invention, show the picture they have drawn, and explain what it is used for and what its advantages are. Investors should ask questions about the inventions, take notes, and draw pictures in the boxes on the next page. Play both roles with several different partners.

Situation: Inventor trying to sell your invention to an investor

Roles: Inventor   Investor

Model Conversation

Inventor: Hi … I'd like to tell you about my new invention. It's called a _____.

Investor: OK. What's it used for?

Inventor: It's used for ___(ing verb)_____.

Investor: Can you describe it?

Inventor: Sure. Look at this picture. It's ___(describe invention)___.

Investor: Why is this invention so special?

Inventor: ___(tell advantages)_____.

Investor: OK. I'll think about it and get back to you.

You, Inventor for the Future

Activity V **Discussion — Which Invention to Invest in?**

Task *Get together with two or three classmates and tell them about the inventions you have seen. Then pretend you are Investors with 100,000 yen that you would like to invest in an exciting new invention. Discuss the inventions you have seen and decide which you will invest in.*

Your Classmates' Cool Inventions

Notes _____

How much will you invest? _____

Notes _____

How much will you invest? _____

Notes _____

How much will you invest? _____

Notes _____

How much will you invest? _____

Units 11 & 12

Task

*The activities below will help you review and reflect on (think about) what you have learned in **Units 11** and **12**.*

1. What useful new words, conversational expressions, or grammar/usage patterns did you learn from the textbook, your teacher, or your classmates?

   _____ _____ _____ _____
   _____ _____ _____ _____
   _____ _____ _____ _____
   _____ _____ _____ _____
   _____ _____ _____ _____

2. Write sentences of your own using the new words, conversational expressions, or grammar/usage patterns you wrote above.

   _____
   _____
   _____
   _____
   _____
   _____

3. What else did you learn in this class about language, culture, etc.?

Unit 13: You and Older People in Your Life

Activity I Discuss the Topic

Task *Read and think about the questions below. Make up one question of your own. Write short answers in the spaces, and then discuss the questions in pairs or small groups.*

1. What older people do you know? Grandparents? Neighbors? Local shop owners? Co-workers at a part-time job?

2. How many grandparents do you have? How often do you see them? Where do they live?

3. What other older people do you know? Where do you know them from?

4. What do you talk about with your grandparents or the other older people you know? Have they ever given you advice? Do they talk about the "old days" when they were young? Do they ever talk about the "war years" (World War II)? Do they ever criticize young people today? If so, what do they say?

5. How do your grandparents and the other older people you know spend their time? What are their hobbies and interests?

6. What problems do older people have? What special needs do they have?

7. Your Question _____

Activity II Getting Ready — Interview Questions

Task 1 Before your next class you need to interview a grandparent or another older person you know. To help you get ready, think of five questions that you would like to ask this person. You can tell them you're doing the interview for a class assignment, so it is a good chance to ask questions you might usually be too shy to ask. You can ask about the person's younger days, first love, the war years, marriage, present life, and so on. Write your questions below.

Your Interview Questions

1. _____
2. _____
3. _____
4. _____
5. _____

Task 2 Get together with two or three other students and compare your interview questions. Which of your group members' questions do you like best? Write them below.

Your Group Members' Interview Questions

1. _____
2. _____
3. _____
4. _____
5. _____

Activity III   Time to Talk — Interviewing an Older Person

Task Now it's time to do the interview (either in person or by telephone). Ask the older person the interview questions you wrote in **Activity II**, as well as any other questions that you think of while doing the interview. Take notes, or if possible, record the interview with your smartphone. In the space below, write up a report of the interview as soon as you can after the interview. Be sure to put in a lot of details.

Useful Language 27

I interviewed ___(name)___ on ___(date)___ at ___(place)___.
He/She is my ___(grandparent, neighbor, friend)___.
I asked him/her ….
She/he told me ….
I thought it was interesting that ….
Today I learned ….
I didn't know that ….
At the end of the interview I thought/felt ….

Your Interview Report

Activity IV — Discuss the Interviews with your Group

Task: Get together with two or three classmates. Tell your group members what you learned from your interview. Don't just read your Interview Report! Try to tell the group about your interview from memory with your book closed. Answer any questions your group interview members might have. Then, when it's your turn to listen to your group members' reports, take notes — and ask questions, too. Finally, write a short summary of each member's interview report.

Interview 1 – Summary

Interview 2 – Summary

Interview 3 – Summary

Unit 14

You, Making Your Own Role Play

Activity I Discuss the Topic

Task *Read and think about the questions below. Make up one question of your own. Write short answers in the spaces, and then discuss the questions in pairs or small groups.*

1. Think of all the different role plays and discussions you have done in this class. Which ones were the most useful to you?

2. Which role plays and discussions were the most fun?

3. Were there any role plays or discussions that you didn't like? If so, what didn't you like about them?

4. What role-play situations did you **not** do in class that you think would be useful or fun to do? Write down three situations on the lines below. Think about the situations, not in this textbook, you might find yourself in when traveling abroad and want to get ready for.

   1) _____
   2) _____
   3) _____

Activity II Getting Ready — Creating Your Own Role Play

Task 1 Get together with two or three other students. Discuss the different role play situations you wrote about in **Activity I** Question 4. Decide on one role play situation you will create a role play for. First, write down the situation and the roles you will play in the box below. Then write down why the people in the role play are talking to each other and what problems they have to solve.

Your Role Play Idea

Situation (place): _____

Roles: _____   _____

 _____   _____

Problems/Reasons for having a conversation

1. _____
2. _____
3. _____
4. _____
5. _____

You, Making Your Own Role Play

Task 2 *Now make up your own **Useful Language** or **Model Conversation** for this role play. If you need help, use a dictionary or ask your teacher. Write it in the box below.*

Useful Language – Model Conversation

Activity III — Role Play — Doing Your Own Role Play

Task *First, do your role play several times in your group. Make sure each member plays all the roles. Then one person should stay behind and the others should join another group. The person who stays behind must explain the role play and go over the **Useful Language** or **Model Conversation** with the new members. Next, practice the role play, switching roles. Make sure that all group members get a chance to visit and do role plays with other groups. Use the boxes on the next page to write down information about the different role plays you do.*

Other Groups' Role Plays

Group 1

Situation (Place): _____

Roles: _____   _____

_____   _____

Problems: _____

_____

Useful Language you want to remember: _____

_____

Group 2

Situation (Place): _____

Roles: _____   _____

_____   _____

Problems: _____

_____

Useful Language you want to remember: _____

_____

Group 3

Situation (Place): _____

Roles: _____   _____

_____   _____

Problems: _____

_____

Useful Language you want to remember: _____

_____

Role Play Evaluation Activities

Here are some ways to evaluate a role play:

1. Your teacher can watch your group do the role play and give you feedback.

2. Your group can watch another group do their role play and give them feedback.

3. You can take a video of your role play and then watch the video and evaluate the role play using the questions below.

Role Play Self-Evaluation Form

1. How was your voice? Was it too loud, too soft, too flat? How could you improve your speaking voice?

2. How was your pronunciation? Did you pronounce all the words carefully and clearly, or did you speak too fast? How could you improve your pronunciation?

3. How was your body language? Did you use gestures to make your communication clearer? Did you make eye contact? What could you do to improve your use of body language?

4. How was your grammar?

    What grammar mistakes did you make and how would you correct them? List the mistakes and correct them, as in the example.

    Example: How much <u>costs</u> the dress? ➡ How much does the dress cost?

5. How was your vocabulary?

    What mistakes did you make with vocabulary and how would you correct them? List your mistakes and correct them as you did in Question 4.

    Example: I worked as a home teacher. ➡ I worked as a tutor.

6. What things did you want to say but did not know the correct English words for? Look up the Japanese words in a dictionary and then list them and their English words below.

7. What else did you learn doing your role play? Write your comments below.

Units 13 & 14

> **Task**
>
> The activities below will help you review and reflect on (think about) what you have learned in **Units 13** and **14**.

1. What useful new words, conversational expressions, or grammar/usage patterns did you learn from the textbook, your teacher, or your classmates?

   _____   _____   _____   _____

   _____   _____   _____   _____

   _____   _____   _____   _____

   _____   _____   _____   _____

   _____   _____   _____   _____

2. Write sentences of your own using the new words, conversational expressions, or grammar/usage patterns you wrote above.

   _____

   _____

   _____

   _____

   _____

   _____

   _____

3. What else did you learn in this class about language, culture, etc.?

Unit 15

Review and Practice

Activity 1 — Can You? – Discussion and Role Play Review Game

Task: Play this game with a partner or another pair to review the discussions and role plays you have done in this class.

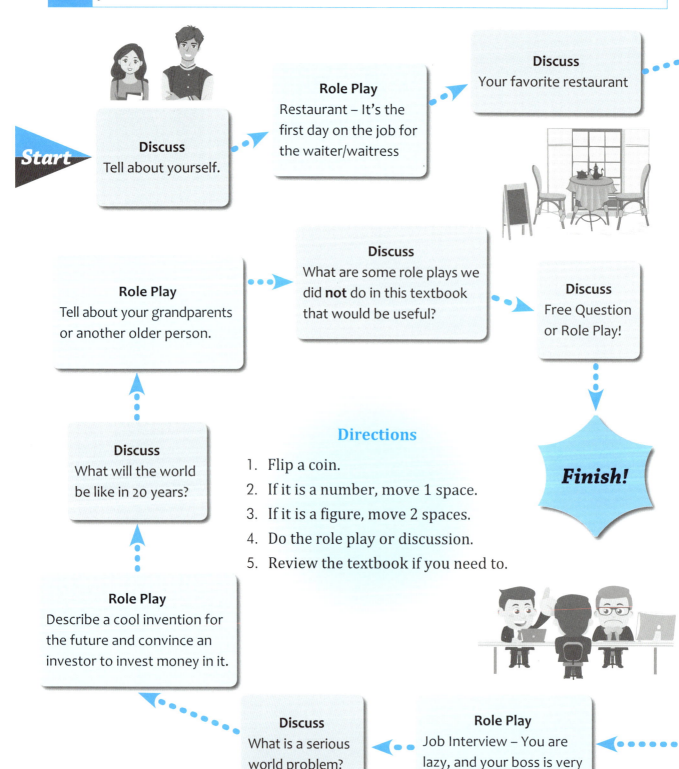

Start

Discuss — Tell about yourself.

Role Play — Restaurant – It's the first day on the job for the waiter/waitress

Discuss — Your favorite restaurant

Discuss — What are some role plays we did **not** do in this textbook that would be useful?

Discuss — Free Question or Role Play!

Role Play — Tell about your grandparents or another older person.

Discuss — What will the world be like in 20 years?

Role Play — Describe a cool invention for the future and convince an investor to invest money in it.

Discuss — What is a serious world problem?

Role Play — Job Interview – You are lazy, and your boss is very strict about everything.

Finish!

Directions
1. Flip a coin.
2. If it is a number, move 1 space.
3. If it is a figure, move 2 spaces.
4. Do the role play or discussion.
5. Review the textbook if you need to.

Role Play
Shopping – You are shopping for shoes.

Discuss
Your favorite store

Role Play
Plan together for a night out on the town.

Discuss
A trip you want to take in Japan.

Role Play
Travel Agency – Convince a customer to take a tour you have planned.

Discuss
Which is the best – a hotel, ryokan, or minshuku?

Role Play
Hotel – Make a reservation to stay in a hotel in Shanghai for New Years.

Discuss
Problems you can have when you travel abroad and how to avoid them.

Role Play
Airline Check-in Counter – Your flight was canceled and you have to be at a wedding tomorrow.

Role Play
Talk to your roommate – He always leaves the room messy.

Discuss
Are you an easy person to live with?

Discuss
What is your dream job?

Review and Practice

Activity II Vocabulary Review

Task Match the English words and expressions on the left with the Japanese on the right.

Vocabulary Review Units 1-3

1.	nationality	_____	a. 顧客
2.	recommend	_____	b. せっかちな
3.	value	_____	c. 雰囲気
4.	atmosphere	_____	d. 国籍
5.	customer	_____	e. 前菜
6.	appetizer	_____	f. 優柔不断な
7.	rude	_____	g. 値打ち
8.	impatient	_____	h. 外観
9.	indecisive	_____	i. 独自の
10.	unique	_____	j. 勧める
11.	advertisement	_____	k. 失礼な
12.	appearance	_____	l. 広告

Vocabulary Review Units 4-6

1.	location	_____	a. 海外へ
2.	sightseeing	_____	b. 場所
3.	curfew	_____	c. 観光
4.	destination	_____	d. 予約
5.	accommodation	_____	e. うるさい
6.	advantage	_____	f. 性別
7.	reservation	_____	g. 宿泊施設
8.	noisy	_____	h. 解決
9.	negotiate	_____	i. 行先
10.	solution	_____	j. 利点
11.	abroad	_____	k. 交渉する
12.	gender	_____	l. 門限

Vocabulary Review Units 7-8

1. supervisor _____
2. immigration _____
3. illegal _____
4. complaint _____
5. apologize _____
6. conservative _____
7. liberal _____
8. lazy _____
9. shy _____
10. considerate _____
11. generous _____
12. refrigerator _____

a. 出入国管理
b. 保守的な
c. 謝る
d. 内気な
e. 思いやりのある
f. 違法の
g. 気前のよい
h. 冷蔵庫
i. 苦情
j. 怠惰な
k. 監督者
l. 進歩的な

Vocabulary Review Units 9-12

1. part-time job _____
2. interview _____
3. quit _____
4. punctual _____
5. creative _____
6. stylish _____
7. advice _____
8. formal _____
9. poverty _____
10. illiterate _____
11. invention _____
12. investor _____

a. 時間に正確な
b. 助言
c. 貧困
d. 発明
e. アルバイト
f. 文盲の
g. おしゃれな
h. 面接
i. 投資家
j. 創造的な
k. 正式な
l. 辞める

For further English practice,
use the website found at:

http://www.ericbray.com/eric-brays-english-study-resource-online

Eric Bray's English Study Resources Online

Listening

Pronunciation

Reading

Chat Opportunities

Grammar

Culture

Dictionaries

Quizzes and Games

Feedback

著作権法上、無断複写・複製は禁じられています。

Starting Off with Role Play and Discussion　　　　　　　　　　[B-878]
これからの英語コミュニケーション講座

| 1　刷 | 2019年4月1日 |
| 5　刷 | 2024年3月29日 |

著　者	エリック・ブレイ　　Eric Bray
発行者	南雲　一範　　Kazunori Nagumo
発行所	株式会社　南雲堂
	〒162-0801　東京都新宿区山吹町361
	NAN'UN-DO Co., Ltd.
	361 Yamabuki-cho, Shinjuku-ku, Tokyo 162-0801, Japan
	振替口座：00160-0-46863
	TEL: 03-3268-2311（営業部：学校関係）
	03-3268-2384（営業部：書店関係）
	03-3268-2387（編集部）
	FAX: 03-3269-2486
編集者	加藤　敦
組　版	柴崎　利恵
装　丁	銀　月　堂
検　印	省　略
コード	ISBN978-4-523-17878-1　　C0082

Printed in Japan

E-mail : nanundo@post.email.ne.jp
URL : https://www.nanun-do.co.jp/